Season of Thanksgiving

A 25 Day Celebration of Gratitude

Jeffrey C. Lilienthal

Season of Thanksgiving

A Twenty-Five Day Celebration of Gratitude

Credits

Cover, book design, and artwork by Terri Morris
(McClearen Design Studio)

Written and edited by Jeffrey C. Lilienthal

Scripture quotations are from the Holy Bible, New King James Version, New American Standard Bible, and New Revised Standard Version.
Copyright © 1984 Thomas Nelson Publishing,
Copyright © 1999 Zondervan Corp.,
Copyright © 1991 Oxford University Press, respectively.

Library of Congress Cataloging-in-Publication Data
Lilienthal, Jeffrey C., 2009

Season of Thanksgiving:
A Twenty-Five Day Celebration of Gratitude / by Jeffrey C. Lilienthal

ISBN 0-61532-775-3

1. Family - Prayer books and devotions - English

2. Non-fiction family bible and inspiration - English

Printed in the United States of America by Lightning Source, Inc., 1246 Heil Quaker Blvd. , Lavergne, TN 37086

Table of Contents

DEDICATION

Season of Thanksgiving is dedicated to our Lord and Savior Jesus Christ who is worthy of all honor, glory, and thanks!

THANKS

With heartfelt gratitude I would like to acknowledge my parents, Alfred and Aileen Lilienthal, whose love and guidance throughout my life have been truly priceless! You are the best parents in the world! I want to thank my siblings Alfred Jr., Kathi, and Heidi as well for a lifetime of love and faithfulness. Each of you is a special gift from God.

I also want to thank my lovely wife, Ronda, for your steadfast love and encouragement throughout all these many years of our marriage. And finally, I want to thank my four wonderful daughters, Annie Lynn, Casey Marie, Kimberly Renee, and Laura Elizabeth who constantly remind me of the goodness of God as revealed in the miracle of each of your lives!

BRIEF DESCRIPTION

Many families, even Christian families, in our country today have adopted an attitude of entitlement that is eroding the very integrity of their relationships with God and others. With a consumeristic appetite that never seems satisfied or content, many of us "honor God with our lips, but our hearts are far away from Him." *Season of Thanksgiving* takes us back to the original intent behind the Thanksgiving holiday: to live a life of heartfelt gratitude before God, recognizing His unmerited grace and our continual dependence upon Him! Through a series of daily devotionals or reflections culminating on Thanksgiving day, young and old alike are invited to experience the deepest treasures of gratitude and praise, allowing God to change our hearts and bring renewed communion with Him and each other.

ABOUT THE AUTHOR

As a deeply committed man of faith, Jeff Lilienthal has been finding ways to express gratitude and praise to God for years (ie. stories, songs, etc.). Having been brought through some significant trials, he recognized long ago that not only is God the source of his talent and creativity, but the source of literally everything of value, including life itself. Realizing the need for authentic heartfelt thankfulness to become much more of a lifestyle in his own family, Jeff began to assemble short devotional "lessons" around this topic that would culminate with the traditional Thanksgiving day celebration. *Season of Thanksgiving: A 25-Day Celebration of Gratitude* for families and singles was the eventual result.

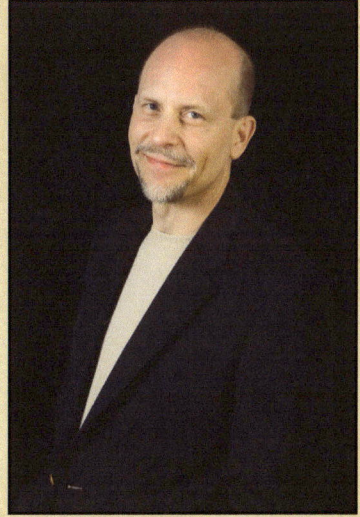

A mental health therapist and adjunct professor at Trevecca Nazarene University, Jeff currently teaches Adult Development classes for TNU's Management and Human Relations Division. The father of four wonderful daughters, he and his wife, Ronda, are members of Trevecca Community Church of the Nazarene and serve in the choir and orchestra. Jeff and his family reside in the rural community of Hendersonville, TN, just north of Nashville.

Introduction

PART ONE

The first Thanksgiving in the new world

When many of the first Pilgrims sailed to the New World in 1620, they brought with them not only hopes and dreams for the future, but a strong faith in God and a precious Christian heritage. On November 11th of that same year, forty-one men, as heads of their households, came together and signed the Mayflower Compact, a covenantal document declaring their commitment to live as God directed. Confident that Divine Providence had led them to this New World, they agreed to live by Christian principles as set forth in the Bible, and by the rule |of law which came from the hand of God.

These Pilgrims, who came primarily from England, landed in the northeastern part of what is now Massachusetts at a place known as Cape Cod. Not far from there they discovered a site where the land was rich and fertile and named it after Plymouth, England. They also decided that it was an ideal place to build a settlement.

The first winter in Plymouth was very hard and many became sick and died. But these people were not like other settlers. The harder things got, the more they prayed and trusted God. Thankfully winter passed and the Pilgrims welcomed spring. One day in March, they were surprised to see just one lone Indian walking up the main road toward the common house (a place where they stayed until their individual homes were built).

When the Indian reached the door, he stopped and said in a deep, booming voice "Welcome!" The Pilgrims were speechless. This Indian spoke English! Finally, they collected themselves and were able to reply "Welcome!" Then they gathered around this tall, well-built stranger and listened as he spoke.

He explained that his name was Samoset, and that he had learned English from fishing captains along the shores of Maine. "I now stay with the Wampanoags who live fifty miles from here" said Samoset. "Their chief, Massasoit, rules over a number of tribes in the area." He went on to describe how some of the white men and some tribes of Indians were hostile to each other, while others were very friendly. But as it was getting late, Samoset requested to sleep in their camp and return to Massasoit in the morning. The Pilgrims agreed.

Although the Indian seemed harmless, they decided to keep a silent watch on Samoset through the night. But the Indian slept soundly and didn't bother anyone. The next morning, the Pilgrims gave him gifts to take to Massasoit as an act of friendship. The following Thursday Samoset returned, this time accompanied by another Indian who also spoke English. But this Indian was a Patuxet.

The Pilgrims listened intently as this new visitor, named Squanto, told his story. Through a number of strange events, Squanto had been captured and eventually sold as a slave to kind Spanish monks. As it turned out, the monks taught Squanto about Jesus and His love for him, all of which prepared the Indian for the important role he would later play at Plymouth settlement.

Upon returning to the New World years later, Squanto learned that nearly all of his people had died, some from disease and others from attack by hostile tribes. Fortunately, Squanto met Massasoit who showed him much kindness. Massasoit was a man of peace who welcomed not only Samoset and Squanto, but also the Pilgrims to Cape Cod. And Massasoit was probably one of the only Indian chiefs who would have done this. But unlike the settlers at Jamestown, the Pilgrims did not make trouble with the Indians. They treated Massasoit and his warriors with respect and showed them the love of Christ.

After Massasoit left the Pilgrim settlement, Squanto remained. "I would like to stay," he said. "My people are gone and I have no one now. I can teach you many things." So, Squanto taught the Pilgrims how to plant corn, stalk deer, plant pumpkins, and make maple syrup. He showed them which herbs to eat, which to use for medicine, and also introduced them to the beaver trade. They considered Squanto a gift from God.

Soon a ship piloted by Captain Jones was to return to England. But the Pilgrims just stood on the shore and watched as the Mayflower sailed away. Not one of them sailed back with him! Although they had lost many loved ones during the winter, they wanted to stay at Plymouth. Something special had happened to them. They had suffered together and had shared the love of Christ with one another. Now, they were truly a family and would not separate.

During the summer of 1621, the Pilgrims worked hard building more houses and trading with the Indians. That fall, they harvested more than enough crops to see them through the winter. In October, Governor William Bradford declared a day of public thanksgiving. The Pilgrims were filled with thanks to Squanto and the Wampanoags who had been so friendly, and to God who had delivered them from certain death! They invited Massasoit, who came with ninety of his warriors and plenty of deer and turkeys. The Pilgrim women cooked fresh vegetables and baked fruit pies and the Indians introduced the settlers to popcorn and other native treats. It was a wonderful time of prayer and rejoicing. The Pilgrims thanked God for meeting their needs and the joyous celebration lasted for three days!

PART TWO

Thanksgiving today and the story
behind this devotional guide

It wasn't until I revisited the story of the first Thanksgiving that it really began to sink in: Our forefathers, the Pilgrims, lived a life of gratitude to God long before that first three day celebration in 1621. Although they experienced times of real hardship, the Pilgrims nevertheless expressed their faith through a nearly continual outpouring of gratitude. And not just some sort of undefinable gratitude or vague sense of thanks; it was a sincere, heartfelt gratitude to the God who had brought them through every trial. They had lost many of their own to be sure and considered life itself a very precious gift, but their trust in God remained firm. And so, as they prepared the turkeys, fish, venison, corn, etc. for that first Thanksgiving feast, their hearts had long since prepared them for the abundance of gratitude that they would once again offer up to God on that first Thanksgiving day.

Fast-forward 388 years. Now with the sounds of football on TV in the next room here we, as a nation, sat (preppy pull-over sweaters and all) about to stuff our faces with turkey, muttering something about being thankful. And yes, I suppose that our country was thankful. On that Thanksgiving day in November of 2002, I know that my family and I were truly thankful. In light of the September 11, 2001 events, we were especially thankful just to be alive and together. Then why, I wondered, do we as a nation wait until Thanksgiving day to "officially" declare out gratitude? And how sincere are we, really? Has Thanksgiving become nothing more than merely a day to chow down on turkey and overdose on sports?

Consider that during the month of December, we as Christians eagerly anticipate the arrival of Christmas day through the experience of a joyous advent season. Advent means "the coming of the Son of God in human form, the Incarnation through the Virgin birth." Believers everywhere attend concerts and other celebrations that harken the birth of our Lord and Savior, Jesus Christ. We don't just wake up one morning, yawn, and say "Oh... hummmm. I guess it's Christmas day." (Or at least we shouldn't!)

While I realize that on one level Thanksgiving may not carry the significance of the Christmas holiday, the whole idea of Thanksgiving does provide us with the perfect prelude, a gateway if you will, to the advent of Jesus Christ. So, on that Thanksgiving day a few years ago, the thought came to me:
Why can't we explore the deeper meanings of Thanksgiving and spend more time allowing the seeds of gratitude to bloom in our hearts? Why can't we, as the Pilgrims did, cultivate a lifestyle of thankfulness, remembering how God through Jesus Christ forgave us and extended His grace to us all who are so undeserving?

Although I initially began this project on thankfulness for my family and I, it was questions like these that eventually led to the devotional you have before you. *Season of Thanksgiving* is intended to help you and your family focus on different aspects of thankfulness during the 25 days leading up to, and including, Thanksgiving day. There are different devotional vignettes, questions for discussion, and optional children's activities for each of the 25 days of the celebration. But just as important, there's a prayer and an action step for each day, one thing each member of the family is willing to do to demonstrate gratitude that day.

It is my sincere belief and prayer that through this devotional guide, you and your family will experience Thanksgiving in a new and vital way. I think you'll find that not only will the turkey taste better, but that a much deeper level of gratitude will be realized, and that you and your family will be ready, as perhaps never before, for the coming advent season as your hearts overflow with a *Season of Thanksgiving!*

PART THREE:

A word or two about using your

Season of Thanksgiving celebration guide

The first thing to keep in mind about *Season of Thanksgiving* is that there are no hard-and-fast rules for use and that it's meant to be a flexible devotional guide for you and your family. We've designed this guide so that the 25th vignette should fall on, or near, Thanksgiving day. However, since the Thanksgiving holiday is always on the fourth Thursday of November, the actual date will change from year to year. For example, in 2009, Thanksgiving will fall on November 26th. But next year, and years thereafter, it might fall on November 23rd, 24th, or even the 25th, depending on when the fourth Thursday actually occurs. We just suggest that, if possible, you begin the 25-day journey so that the last devotional corresponds with Thanksgiving day itself. (If you were to do this in 2009, you would obviously need to begin on November 2nd.) Again, this is only a suggestion! We want you to do what will work best in your given situation.

Moreover, this guide is intended for singles as well as married folk with or without children. Some singles may find it helpful to use the guide as part of a Sunday school class, etc. where they can interact around the devotional content. Although the children's activities can be optional, some adults may find certain ones to be helpful and even fun! Again, no hard-and-fast rules apply.

Finally, and most importantly, please remember the main reason for going through *Season of Thanksgiving*: to offer up praises to God from our hearts, to express gratitude and to bless others with the words and actions of thankfulness. And by focusing on the many facets of giving thanks, to prepare our hearts for the joyous advent season to come! This is why this devotional guide exists...to bless you and your family as we enter this special holiday season. As mentioned earlier in the introduction, we don't want Thanksgiving to devolve into only a day of food, sports, and parades. When Thanksgiving day arrives, we want your hearts to be prepared (as well as your stomachs) to truly celebrate this special day. Thank you, and may God richly bless you and your family!

What does the word Thanksgiving mean?

"...and he took the seven loaves and the fish; and giving thanks,
He broke them and started giving them to the disciples,
and the disciples gave them to the people" (Matt. 15:36, NASB)

Random House defines thanksgiving as "the act of giving thanks" or "an expression of thanks, especially to God." In our scripture reference from Matthew, we see Jesus giving thanks to God the Father before dividing the loaves and fishes and before the miracle feeding of over 4,000 people. If our Lord and Savior took the time to express thanks to the heavenly Father, how much more should we follow His example!

Over the next twenty-five days or so, leading up to Thanksgiving Day, we will be learning more about what it means to be truly thankful. We will be looking at why some people are thankful, why others are not, and why being thankful makes such a big difference to everyone, especially God. So, if thanksgiving means *the act of giving thanks...* let's talk about it.

Let's Talk About It!

1) What are some "acts" that could be examples of giving thanks?
2) Can you think of some things you've seen your friends do to show thanks?
3) Why do you think Jesus expressed thanks to God?

Children's Activity

(Suggested Supplies: large poster board or construction paper, broad tip washable markers, crayon or ink pen, tape or refrigerator magnets)

1) Near the top of the poster board or construction paper, using the broad tip markers, write the words "Thank you, God, for..." (in large letters).
2) Using a crayon or ink pen, write two or three things on the poster that you're thankful for.
3) Parents, help your child put the poster up in a place where the family can see it every day (ie. refrigerator, kitchen wall, etc.)

Prayer...

Dear God, by our words and our actions, help each one of us express thankfulness to You every day.

Action Step

(This is a continuation of the children's activity.)

Every day through Thanksgiving Day, have each member of the family add two or three things to the poster that he or she is thankful for. If you can't think of three things, at least add one each day. These could be material blessings, like a toy, or they could be things like good health, safety, or peace in the middle of a difficult situation. If you want, you could leave the poster up and keep adding to it after Thanksgiving Day. We suggest that you save the poster, perhaps bringing it out at certain times, to remind you of God's goodness in your lives.

Day 2

When do people usually act thankful?

"Little children, let us not love with word or with tongue, but in deed and truth." (1 John 3:18, NASB)

It was Christmas day and everyone was opening presents. I was about nine years old and was expecting some sort of "super-duper" toy from my grandparents. (I think I had asked for some kind of toy gun.) When it was my turn to open my gift, I was shocked to discover that they had bought clothes for me instead! Trying to hide my disappointment, I mustered a fake smile and sheepishly said, "Oh thank you Nana and Grandpa!"

That Christmas morning I was expected to be thankful, although I knew it wasn't sincere. Admittedly, it wasn't very loving of me to just "act" thankful, because God wants our actions and words to be right and true. As we grow older, let us allow God's Spirit to make us truly grateful for all things... big *and* small.

Let's Talk About It!

1) Name some occasions when we are expected to "act" thankful.

2) Can you think of a time when you were expected to be grateful, but you weren't?

3) Do you think you should "act" thankful when you're really not thankful? Why or why not?

Children's Activity

(Suggested Supplies: plain or colored construction paper, washable markers or crayons, safety scissors, safety pin)

1) Parents please help your child make a small sign about the size of a name tag that reads
"IT'S NO ACT! I'M THANKFUL FOR_____"

2) Parents, help your child complete the statement by filling in the blank.

3) Cut the sign out and affix the safety pin so that later the sign can be worn on a shirt.

Prayer

{ *Dear God, please help us ALL to be truly thankful, even for the little things or things we may not prefer (like Brussels sprouts).*

Action Step

Over the next few days, encourage each other to be grateful, especially for seemingly small, insignificant things. If someone complains (ie. at the dinner table about some food he/she doesn't like) gently remind him/her about the family's focus on thankfulness for little things. If the person apologizes and says "I guess I am thankful after all," ask him/her to wear the sign that was made during the children's activity. The bottom line is that we need to not only act like we're thankful, we need to be thankful!

Day 3

The Fruit of Our Lips

"Through Him then, let us continually offer up a sacrifice of praise to God, that is, the fruit of lips that give thanks to His name." (Heb. 13:15, NASB)

God, the master designer, has fashioned our vocal instruments in such a way as to allow for a nearly infinite variety of sounds and voice inflections. We can hum, whistle, shout, and even sing!

Given all of these options, we face an even bigger decision, and the choice is up to each one of us: we can choose to praise the name of our Lord or we can choose to curse our brother. With the same mouth we can offer gifts of praise and encouragement or we can hurt others and even grieve the heart of God.

The writer of Hebrews encourages us to continually offer up the sacrifice of praise... the fruit of our lips. It is a sacrifice because we must willfully choose to praise instead of curse. And what comes to mind when we think of "fruit?" Something sweet, refreshing, and nutritious! When our praise is sincere, it is sweet, refreshing, and nourishing to our Lord. So, let us continually offer praise to our heavenly Father, for He indeed is worthy of ever-lasting thanks!

Let's Talk About It!

1) What do you usually find flowing out of your mouth, praises or curses? Gifts of encouragement?

2) Are your words sweet, like fruit? Or, are they repulsive, more like moldy garbage?

3) What can you do to keep praises and words of encouragement upon your lips instead of curses?

Children's Activity

(Suggested supplies: colored construction paper, ie. yellow, red, green, etc., a dark washable marker or crayon, safety scissors, tape.)

1) Have your child draw various shapes of fruit on the construction paper (e.g. banana on the yellow, etc.)

2) Ask your child to write one or two sweet words inside of a sweet-tasting fruit. (Parents might need to help with this.) For example, inside of a sweet fruit like a peach, you could write the words "You're Wonderful!"

3) Then, ask your child to write one or two sour or yucky words inside of the "sour-tasting" fruit. For example, inside of a sour fruit like a lemon, you could write the words "You stink!"

4) Explain that when we thank God or encourage others, it's like giving them a delicious bowl of fruit! They love it!

5) Say to your child: "Let's give God a bowl of delicious fruit. Let's praise His name!"

6) Sing a song of praise with your child (their choice).

Prayer

Dear Jesus, help me remember to always praise your wonderful name! May the fruit of my lips be pleasing to You and encouraging to others. Amen.

Action Step

Place the fruit shapes your children made with sweet and sour words on them in an envelope. At the end of the week, ask each member of the family to select one fruit from the envelope that best represents his or her words from the past week. The same fruit may be used by more than one family member. For example, dad might select a "rotten apple" with the word "nasty" inside because he believes his words were rather "nasty" during the past week. One at a time, each person selects a fruit from the envelope and says: "I've chosen a _____ ie. banana, grape, etc. because I think my words this past week were _____ (ie. nasty, wonderful, super, etc.). The object of this exercise is to be honest with each other about the "fruit of our lips," to apologize when necessary, and to ask God to help us do better. It is also an opportunity to thank each other for words of praise and encouragement, if that's in order.

Alternative for Singles or Married without Children

You can accomplish a similar action step as above by simply thinking of a fruit and words to go with it. The important thing is to admit to your spouse or a trusted friend the exact nature of your attitude, the "fruit of your lips," during the past week. If your fruit, your words weren't so good, be honest about it. Pray for each other and offer encouragement to do better, if that's appropriate.

Day 4

Are you thankful from the heart?

"Now one of them, when he saw that he had been healed, turned back, glorifying God with a loud voice." (Luke 17:15, NASB)

In the 17th chapter of Luke, there is a story about ten lepers who were all healed by Jesus. But only one was deeply moved with gratitude. In fact, he "threw himself at Jesus' feet and thanked Him." By contrast, we are told about a man in Matthew chapter 18 who was very ungrateful. This man owed the king "ten thousand talents" (a lot of money) and was about to be sold, along with his wife, children, and all his possessions, to repay the debt. But when he fell on his knees and begged for mercy, the king "took pity on him, canceled the debt and let him go."

No sooner was the man freed when he found one of his coworkers who owed him "a hundred denarii" (very little money). He grabbed him by the throat and demanded that he be paid back immediately! His fellow worker fell to his knees and begged for mercy. "Be patient with me and I will pay you back," he cried. But the man refused and had his coworker thrown into prison.

When the king heard about this, he became very angry. "Shouldn't you have had mercy on your fellow worker," shouted the king, "just as I had mercy on you?" And in disgust, he threw the man into jail until every penny would be paid.

Let's Talk About It

1) In the first story, why do you think only one man returned to thank Jesus for healing him?

2) Do you think the man in the second story was truly thankful that the king forgave his enormous debt? Why or why not?

3) Can you think of a time when your heart was filled with gratitude toward God or someone else? Did you try to express your thankfulness?

4) How can you tell if someone is really thankful, from the heart?

Children's Activity

(Suggested supplies: two pieces of plain or colored construction paper, washable markers / crayons, safety scissors)

1) Using one at a time, position a piece of paper horizontally.

2) Fold in half, from left to right.

3) Starting at the fold near the top, draw an "ear-shaped" line back to the fold, near the bottom.

4) Cut out along the "ear-shaped" line and open the paper to reveal a heart shape.

5) Inside one paper heart, draw a picture that shows ingratitude or unthankfulness.

6) Inside the other paper heart, draw a picture that shows real gratitude or thankfulness.

Prayer

Dear God, I pray that I might be deeply touched by your unlimited loving-kindness. Help me to be truly thankful, not only for the kindness of others, but for the gift of salvation. And please help me to express my gratitude from the heart.

Action Step

Parents, please post your child's two paper hearts in a prominent place (such as the refrigerator). During the coming week, use the two hearts as a reminder to keep your attitudes pure, loving, and truly thankful. Share openly about this, not to criticize, but to help each other by admitting fault, forgiving, and by expressing gratitude toward one another.

Day 5

Expect a blessing!

"He who sows sparingly will also reap sparingly, and he who sows bountifully will also reap bountifully. So let each one give as he purposes in his heart, not grudgingly or of necessity; for God loves a cheerful giver." (2 Cor. 9:6-7, NKJV)

In this special season of blessing, one of the greatest privileges we have is the ability to give, to give of our resources, our energies, and ourselves. Some people only think about giving so that they will get back. But I have found that the richest rewards we receive come as a natural result of giving out of a heart of gratitude.

The feeling of joy that comes when we give bountifully and cheerfully is indescribable! And I believe it comes only from the Lord. When we stop to think of all that God has given us, especially the gift of his Son, how can we help but want to give back all that we can? After all, we can never out-give the Lord! And when, from a heart of thanksgiving, we bless our heavenly Father and bless others, we can expect a blessing in return. This blessing may not be a material one, but will certainly be one of joy overflowing!

Let's Talk About It!

1) Why do you think some people are reluctant to give?

2) When you've given a gift or helped someone out, how did that make you feel?

Children's Activity

1) From a thankful heart, what will you give God today?

2) What will you give to others today? (Hint: it could be a gift, or just helping your mom or dad around the house.)

Prayer

{ *Dear Father, because we have freely received, help us to freely give. And let our hearts not grumble or complain, but overflow with sincere gratitude.*

Action Step

Parents take the lead by offering to help out a neighbor or friend today. It could be something very simple like shoveling the snow off of your neighbor's walk, raking their leaves, or babysitting their children so they can have an evening together. In any case, encourage your kids to join in and make it a family project!

Day 6

Why are so many people unthankful?

"...although they knew God, they did not glorify Him as God, nor were thankful, but became futile in their thoughts, and their foolish hearts were darkened." (Rom. 1:21, NKJV)

I recently heard about a professional basketball player who makes around five million dollars a year (not counting endorsements, movies, personal appearance money, etc.) Yet, when he found out that a player on a different team was making $7.5 million to play the same position, he became very indignant. "Can you believe they expect me to live on this?" he complained to the news media. "It isn't fair and I'm not putting up with it!"

In Romans chapter one, verse twenty, we read "For since the creation of the world His [God's] invisible attributes are clearly seen, being understood by the things that are made, so that they are without excuse..." And as mentioned above, we know that many do not recognize or thank God for his provision of life and sustenance.

It's very clear, even to those in the world, that God created everything. So the problem is with us, not Him. Many choose to deny Him, and instead of being thankful for the abundance He has provided, they grumble and complain. We may shake our heads at the pro athlete who gripes about a five million dollar salary, but how we must grieve the heart of God with all our whining and complaining! After all, He has provided not only a country rich in freedom and abundance, but offers his very presence to live and abide within us!

Let's Talk About It

1) Why do you think so many people have unthankful hearts?

2) Is it possible to be thankful with very little, or even nothing at all?

Children's Activity

1) Can you think of a famous person, or a person with great wealth or power, who seems ungrateful? (Write his or her name on a small piece of paper.)

2) By contrast, can you think of someone in poverty whose heart overflows with thanksgiving? (Write his or her name on a small piece of paper.)

Prayer

{ *Dear heavenly Father, help us not to grumble and complain, but instead to dwell on all the riches we possess in Christ Jesus!*

Action Step

Parents, please post the two pieces of paper with the two names on them in a prominent place (such as on the refrigerator). Over the next few days when each family member sees the two pieces of paper, let the names on them serve as reminders to be grateful and NOT to grumble and complain!

Day 7

A Time of Testing

"Consider it all joy, my brethren, when you encounter various trials, knowing that the testing of your faith produces endurance."
(James 1:2-3, NASB)

My mother has always described our time on earth as "a testing time." She believes that God tests our faith with trials to see if we really mean business. James admonishes us to "consider it all joy" when we run into difficult times because the testing of our faith will produce patience. It's amazing, but James is telling us to be thankful, and even joyous, when adversity strikes! But when you stop to think about it, many of our happiest times comes after periods of intense struggle.

Consider the many ways that we challenge ourselves in this society. In the Super Bowl, the two best football teams do battle to see who will be worthy to be called "World Champions." We encourage our children to work hard in school and rise to the top of the class. Companies have sales contests to see who will become "salesperson of the year." We know that nothing of real value comes easily, or without a cost, and so we welcome the challenge. But while we as Christians welcome trails or challenges, we need to face them in a much different way. We need to put our faith in God, and not merely rely on our own talents and abilities!

I think this is why James says to be happy and thankful when trials come, because trials really put our faith to the test. In this way, God can produce patience and character in us. It isn't the easy way, but in this case, it's the best way! Like a musician trying to master an instrument, there are no shortcuts, just long hours of disciplined practice. And every Christian should be thankful that God doesn't take shortcuts with us either. So we can rejoice when trials come, knowing that if we're patient and obedient, God will bring something good out of each and every one.

Let's Talk About It!

1) Describe a time when God used a trial in your life to bring about something good. Now, as you look back on it, are you thankful for the trial?

2) Are you thankful for the difficulties you're going through right now? Why or why not?

Children's Activity

1) Have you and your children "act out" the story of David and Goliath. (Explain that Goliath was a trial for David and the Israelites.)

2) To further clarify, ask your child: "How do you think David would have felt if Goliath had been one foot tall and used a hot-dog as a weapon? (Typical Answers: "He would have laughed; "none of the Israelites would have been afraid," etc.)

3) Then explain that if Goliath had been one foot tall, he would have been no trial for David at all! Explain that a trial is something that is hard or difficult for us.

4) Tell your child that we need to thank God for trials because they make us remember how much we need God's help. We can be thankful for trials (like Goliath) because we know that God will be with us!
(Optional): Sing "I'm in the Lord's Army" with your child. Explain that in "God's army," we go into battle (trials) with God's weapons (such as God's power, prayer, the Bible, praise, etc.)

Prayer

Dear Father, help me to rejoice and give thanks when "Goliaths" (trials) come along. Help me to remember that You will go through every trial, every battle, with me! Help me keep my faith in You strong.

Action Step

Why not put the prayer above into action right now? With your eyes closed, think of a difficult problem you're currently facing. Now place your hands together, palms up, and picture the problem sitting in the middle of your hands. Say a prayer something like this:

"Heavenly Father, thank you for this trial. I know you've allowed it in my life for a reason. But I've been carrying it all alone, without success, and now I give it to You. Thank you for taking this burden and for giving me the strength I couldn't supply on my own. I know that with your grace and power, I can conquer this problem, just like David conquered Goliath. Thank you for loving me enough to allow trials like this into my life! In Jesus' name, Amen."

Day 8

What does it mean to be thankful?

"I will bless the Lord at all times; His praise shall continually be in my mouth." (Ps. 34:1 , NASB)

Over the years, people have given a variety of answers to the question: What does it mean to be thankful? Here are just a few of the possible responses:

"It means I'm very glad for everything I have."

"I realize I don't really deserve what I have."

"Thankfulness makes me want to help others less fortunate, like giving to charities or helping the homeless."

"It means I shouldn't waste so much time griping and complaining!"

"Well, when I think about all that God has forgiven me for, I tend to be a lot less critical of others."

"I think the apostle Paul had it right when he said that whether we have little or much we should learn to be content."

"To me it means that we can praise God no matter what, knowing that regardless of what may happen He is always with us!"

"I'm most thankful for Christ's sacrifice on the cross because even though I don't deserve it, His death and resurrection alone gives me everlasting life in heaven!"

One final thought about thankful people: Even when they are given lemons, they find a way to make lemonade. Thankful people look for the good in others and in situations and try to always find something redeeming. In short, they take on the very attitude of Christ!

Let's Talk About It

1) What does thankfulness mean to you, especially right now... today?

Children's Activity

1) Parents, please help your child make a tangible representation of his/her response to the question above. For example, if your daughter said "Thankfulness means to be happy with the toys I have," you might ask her to draw a picture of those toys.

Prayer

{ *Dear Jesus, help us to remember what it really means to be thankful. And help us wake up each day with truly grateful hearts.*

Action Step

If you'd like, you might display the representation your child made during the children's activity as a reminder of what thankfulness means to you.

Day 9

Live Each Day With an Attitude of Thanksgiving

*"Do not worry about anything, but in everything by prayer
and supplication with thanksgiving let your requests
be made known to God."* (Phil. 4:6, NRSV)

According to this scripture, we should rest in the faithfulness of God to supply every need. We are to make our requests known to God in a very humble way, with thankfulness in our hearts and praises upon our lips. As we talked about before, thankfulness requires us to focus on the goodness of God despite any outward circumstance.

Verse seven in chapter four of Philippians goes on to tell us that if we do these things with sincerity, the peace of God which surpasses all understanding will guard our hearts and minds through Christ Jesus. So we, therefore can take tremendous comfort in this particular promise of God!

I, for one, have lived long enough to know that there will be days of sunshine and days of rain, moments of pleasure and times of pain. My fervent prayer is simply that God will honor us with His presence each and every day, in the midst of any and all circumstances. He may not choose to deliver us from all pain and suffering, but we can give thanks knowing that His grace is more than sufficient for every trial of life!

Let's Talk About It!

1) Can you recall a time when you kept praising God in spite of hardship?

2) Can you name someone from the Bible who kept an attitude of thanksgiving even during terrible adversity?

Children's Activity

1) Sing "Down In My Heart" together (you know…I've got the joy, joy, joy, joy down in my heart, etc.) But first, tell your children we need to keep God's joy in our hearts because other people around us may be grumpy and unthankful.

2) Remember to tell them that God loves those people, too, and so should we! Does your child have his/her smiley face on?

Prayer...

{ *Dear God, we may fall down and get hurt or be sad at times. Help us to remember that You are still with us, giving us Your peace and joy. With You in our hearts, we can be thankful no matter what!*

Action Step

Can your family think of at least one prayer request that you have had a hard time submitting to God with thanksgiving and supplication? Would you be willing to try again, this time thanking God and resting in His faithfulness no matter the outcome?

Day 10

Be thankful for weaknesses?

"I am now rejoicing in my sufferings for your sake…"
(Col. 1:24, NRSV)

The apostle Paul knew what it meant to suffer for the gospel of Christ. Yet, by the grace of God he was able to come to the place where he counted even weaknesses and sufferings as a badge of honor. In 2 Cor. 12:10, Paul wrote "for whenever I am weak, then I am strong," meaning that when his own human strength failed him, the power of God shone even brighter through his life. Paul knew that the great things God was doing through his human frailty could only be accomplished by the power of the Holy Spirit. In fact, Paul became acutely aware that when he relied solely on the strength of God, it was then and only then that the real work of the kingdom could be done.

A significant time of trial and difficulty for me came in 1994. I experienced physical injury and pain as well as emotional and relational challenges. All of these things combined made my already stressful work situation nearly unbearable. I took a leave of absence from full-time counseling and leaned heavily on the Lord for strength, encouragement, and restoration. Now, whenever I think about those days, I thank God for my weaknesses during that time and realize how much I grew in the Lord through those struggles. How true it is that His power is made perfect in our weaknesses!

Let's Talk About It!

1) Can you share a time when you were so tired, weak, or sick that you literally could do nothing of any value?

2) Do you think it's possible to be truly humble when you can do almost anything in your own strength?

3) Why do you think that God does His best work through ordinary, flawed, weak people who are willing to let Him?

Children's Activity

(Suggested supplies: Plain white or colored construction paper, crayons or washable markers, tape.)

1) Briefly remind your child of the story of Moses' birth and how he was rescued from the mighty waters of the Nile river, protected by only a fragile basket of straw, sticks, and mud.

2) Have your child draw a picture of Moses in the basket as it floated down the Nile, exposed to all of the dangers lurking there in the chaotic, turbulent waters.

3) Remind your child that even though the basket was fragile (by human standards), God was there protecting Moses with His mighty hand! (Parents: you may want to display your child's picture as a reminder to be thankful in our weaknesses.)

Prayer

Father, help us all to be thankful for our weaknesses, knowing that your power is made perfect in our frailty. Help us to remember that insults, hardships, struggles, etc. are all opportunities for your power and grace to shine through us to others!

Action Step

If you're willing, have each member of the family think of at least one weakness (human flaw, struggle, etc.) that has been considered an inadequacy or a bad thing up to this point. Perhaps it's something that can't be changed, such as a physical feature or an average intellect. Whatever it is, would you be willing to actually thank God for this "weakness?" Would you be willing to let God use you in spite of this "weakness," realizing that God does so much more through "weak" vessels? Remember Moses? He was anything but an eloquent speaker; in fact, he stuttered! Yet God chose to use Moses to lead the children of Israel out of Egypt. What about you? What could God do through you?

Day 11

We have so much to be thankful for!

"Enter into His gates with thanksgiving, And into His courts with praise. Be thankful to Him, and bless His name. For the Lord is good." (Ps. 100:4, NASB)

Look around you right now. What do you see? Your mother or father? Your spouse, your children? A warm home with fun things to do? How often do you thank the Lord for everything He's given you? He has given us so much, hasn't He!

Well, in case you question the Lord's provision in your life, consider this story as originally told by Chip Ingram (from the *Living On The Edge radio program*). Chip was recalling a visit he made to a Latin American country where he met a fellow that we'll call Juan. A young Christian, Juan was radiant with the joy and gratitude of Christ. Juan offered to take Chip on a little motor-scooter to see Juan's home on the hillside of the city. As they weaved in and out of the chaotic city traffic, Chip remembers praying "Oh Lord, please help us make it there and back in one piece!" But Juan was unflappable, smiling from ear-to-ear as he pointed to a row of make-shift shacks and tiny huts lining the hillside on the outskirts of the city. Juan pointed to one particular shack near the top of a hill that appeared to have an electrical wire running to it. "That's my home," Juan said joyfully.

When they reached the tiny dwelling, Juan took Chip inside and proudly showed him around. "This is where we all sleep," said Juan, still smiling as he pointed to a small area with just one simple cot for a bed. In fact, Chip noticed that the entire house was about the size of a typical one-car garage, with dirt or rough wood floors and, except for one bare light bulb hanging down over the main room, appeared to contain no modern conveniences. Yet, here was Juan, seemingly as happy as could be with the whole situation. "Dear brother Chip," Juan continued, "we are so blessed to be the only home on this hillside with an electric light. Many of our neighbors, who come to our home at night to hear the Bible read to them, are so grateful and encouraged by the message of Christ. And sharing the good news with them touches our hearts as we see many lives changed forever!"

I think Juan represents a great lesson to us all. For instead of griping and complaining about all things he didn't have, Juan decided to be truly thankful for the simple things he did have, especially that one lone light bulb that God used in a powerful way! So, are you truly thankful for everything you have? And even more importantly, are you allowing God to use even the simplest things in your life as a testimony to others of His goodness and grace?

Let's Talk About It!

1) Like Juan, are you truly thankful for everything you have, whether it be little or much?

2) Do you constantly remind yourself that we weren't put here on earth to accumulate lots of stuff? But rather, we are here to glorify God with our lives, to be ministers of reconciliation and agents of grace.

Children's Activity

(Suggested supplies: Drawing paper, crayons or washable markers, scissors)

1) Ask your children to draw a picture of their five favorite things. It could be toys, pets, whatever.

2) Ask them to cut the pictures out with scissors (for use later).

(Please select some object in your home to function as an altar. If they're willing, ask your children to place the pictures of their five favorite things on the "altar" as an act of gratitude and submission. Then, pray the following prayer together.)

Prayer

{ *Dear Jesus, I give you the most important things in my life to use as you desire. In fact, I offer myself as a "living sacrifice," thankful that you might use me to help build your kingdom.*

Action Step

In your family prayer time during the week to come, ask each family member to thank the Lord for at least one thing that he/she has never given thanks for. (It could even be something that he/she wishes would go away, perhaps even a burden.) The idea is to be thankful for even the smallest things (like Juan's light bulb) that God might use for his glory.

Day 12

Not very thankful? Check your pulse!

"Clap your hands, all you peoples; shout to God with loud songs of joy. For the Lord, the Most High, is awesome..."
(Ps. 47:1-2, NRSV)

We hear the word awesome used today to describe everything from toothpaste to rock stars. But in the truest sense, terms such as awesome should be reserved for the One who is, in every way, *awesome.* When we think about God's majesty and grace, his unlimited ability to create universes beyond imagination, and his infinite love, our breath is taken away and we are left literally speechless.

If the proclamation from Paul in Romans 8, verses 38-39 doesn't leave you overwhelmed with thankfulness, you really should check your pulse! Paul states: "For I am convinced that neither death, nor life, nor angels, nor rulers, nor things present, nor things to come, nor powers, nor height, nor depth, nor anything else in all creation, will be able to separate us from the love of God in Christ Jesus our Lord." (NRSV)

Recently, we've all heard about the horrific disasters in Myanmar (cyclone) and China (earthquake) that have claimed thousands of lives. And although in the minority, there were believers in those countries that undoubtedly lost their lives as well. Yet, even with all of the bad news that pummels us on a daily basis it's so amazing to know that God loves us, *all* of us, with an unconditional love that defies human comprehension. Again, although we can't understand it, somehow, someway, God loves us so much that not even death can separate us from his love! If that doesn't bring joy and hope to your heart...you really should check your pulse!

Let's Talk About It!

1) Who might be someone that you could name who loves you very much? (ie. Your mother or father? etc.)

2) Can you think of anything you've done, or could do, that would make them stop loving you?

3) Are you thankful that God loves you so much that nothing will ever make Him stop loving you?

Children's Activity

Parents, show your child how to take a pulse. Then, take turns checking each other's pulse. Discuss with your child what it means to be alive and human. Discuss the fact that because God designed us in his image, we are to be grateful children, thankful for the hope that lies within us…the assurance of eternal life with Him!

Prayer

Heavenly Father, thank you for your unconditional love for us! Thank you that nothing, not even death, will separate us from your love. Amen!

Action Step

(Parents, depending on the age and maturity level of your child, you can decide if you should involve him/her in this action step.) Seek out someone in your church community who has experienced the death of a loved one, but try to find someone whose loss hasn't been too recent. Ask this person if he/she would mind talking with you about the loss and if so, ask if the loved one was a believer. If so, ask the individual to share thoughts or feelings and specifically what it means to know that this loved one went to live with God forever.

Day 13

Go tell it on the mountain!

"O sing unto the Lord a new song; sing to the Lord, all the earth. Sing to the Lord, bless his name; tell of his salvation from day to day. Declare his glory among the nations, his marvelous works among all the peoples." (Ps. 96: 1-3, NRSV)

"Go Tell It on the Mountain," an African-American spiritual dating back to around 1865, has become a well-known Christmas song that encourages people everywhere to spread the good news of Christ's birth in Bethlehem. And there are many, in all nations around the world, whose lives have been so dramatically transformed that they eagerly tell anyone who'll listen about this good news. Paul, of course, was one such man. Recall that on the Damascus road he encountered the risen Christ and was dramatically converted to Christianity. As a result, Paul traveled far and wide to preach the good news of Christ's redeeming grace, the forgiveness of sins, and the hope of eternal life in heaven.

We, too, should reassess our level of enthusiasm about what God has done for us. You might ask yourself "Am I as thankful and excited about telling others as Paul was? Am I so grateful for God's amazing grace that I look for opportunities to share the good news with others?" In truth, we all get so bogged down with the details of everyday life that it becomes easy to lose our zeal. But if we'll just stop for a moment and remember how precious our salvation really is, we may well find ourselves singing the words of that great chorus "Go tell it on the mountain, over the hills and everywhere…go tell it on the mountain that Jesus Christ is born!"

Let's Talk About It!

1) Honesty Time! From a heart of thankfulness, when was the last time you shared the good news of Jesus Christ?

2) If it's been a while, why do you think you haven't shared it with someone?

3) What do you think it will take to reignite your enthusiasm for sharing the gospel?

Children's Activity

Sing the song "Go Tell It On The Mountain" with your children. If you'd like, add in simple household items as percussion instruments (e.g. spoons, shakers, etc.). Make it FUN!

Prayer

Dear Jesus, please light a fire within us once again to help us tell everyone about you! Forgive us for failing to share by becoming so wrapped-up in worldly things. We thank you for your presence and ask you to fill us to overflowing so that we can love others as you commanded. In Jesus' name, Amen.

Action Step

This week, make a new commitment to share the good news of what Christ has done, and is doing, in your life. Over the next couple of weeks, determine to tell at least one other person each day about God's work in your life. And rather than "preaching" at them, try to simply love others by doing kind things for them and by sharing what God is doing for you and in you!

Day 14

Why should we be thankful?

"A joyful heart is good medicine, But a broken spirit dries up the bones." (Prov. 17: 22, NASB)

In the classic tale, *Anne of Avonlea*, there is an unforgettable character named Katherine who is the principal of a school for young women. Katherine is a bitter young woman whose resentment of the past has left her with a truly ungrateful heart. As a result, people shun her, opportunities escape her, and her emotional and physical health are in poor shape as well.

When we have an ungrateful, dismal attitude toward life, we can expect life to have an uncooperative attitude toward us. As with Katherine, people will tend to avoid us, and even our physical health is more likely to decline. On the other hand, when we choose to be grateful for each day of life, truly thankful for what Christ has done (and is doing), then God's peace comes into our hearts and brings health to our bones. Many people have unnecessary sadness, fears, physical aches and pains, not to mention poor relationships, and often it's because of nothing more than an unthankful heart and a miserable attitude.

Although we shouldn't practice thankfulness and joy simply for the benefits, the fact remains that there are numerous rewards that come as a result of choosing to have a grateful heart! Yes, we all experience losses and set-backs, it's true; but a grateful, joyous heart is, indeed, *good medicine!*

Let's Talk About It!

1) Recall the last time you were truly thankful or joyous. How did you feel "deep down in your bones?"

2) Do you think it's possible to be angry or bitter and really thankful at exactly the same time?

3) Who do you think are healthier? Bitter, hateful, resentful people? Or, grateful, joyous, contented people? Why?

Children's Activity

(Suggested supplies: small cup or container of water, pepper, bottle of liquid soap)

1) Begin by sprinkling a small amount of pepper onto the top, center of the cup of water. Let the water represent our lives and the pepper represent a bitter, dismal attitude. Now, let the liquid soap represent the attitude of joy, the good medicine!

2) Squeeze a drop of liquid soap (the "good medicine") onto the middle of the pepper sprinkled on the water. What happened next? That's right, the soap (representing a grateful, joyous attitude) made the bitterness literally "run" in all directions! Bitterness just can't survive when God's joy comes on the scene.

Prayer

Father, help me choose to be thankful and my heart to be joyous even when life is sometimes difficult. Help me to remember that a joyful heart is good medicine. Amen.

Action Step

Set the pepper container and the liquid soap bottle on the dining room table tonight. Over supper, use them as reminders to choose joy and gratitude. You might even want to tell a few jokes; but the important thing is to laugh and enjoy each other's company, allowing the "good medicine" of joy to permeate your spirits.

Day 15

The Greatest Gift of All

"For a child has been born for us, a son given to us; authority rests upon his shoulders; and he is named Wonderful Counselor, Mighty God, Everlasting Father, Prince of Peace." (Is. 9:6, NRSV)

When I stop to consider all the people and things for which I am thankful, the one that goes to the top of the list, the one that outshines them all is the greatest gift of all…the Messiah and redeemer of all mankind: Christ Jesus! A musical masterpiece, the *Messiah*, composed in the summer of 1741, is George Friderick Handel's most famous oratorio and was penned to honor our tiny planet's reception of this Creator and Savior.

As a music major in college, I was required to attend a class entitled Oratorio Chorus. At first I wasn't too interested, but then I discovered that we would be learning the words and music to Handel's Messiah. As we practiced the various harmony parts along with the solos, I think we all became deeply affected by the text taken entirely from the Bible. Handel was inspired as well, constructing glorious melody lines and interweaving harmonies to tell the story of Christ's advent on earth. This is the one we had been waiting for! This child is the King of kings and Lords of lords! He is, in effect, the *greatest gift of all!*

Let's Talk About It!

1) Is there a difference between being offered a gift and actually receiving or accepting that gift?

2) Why is it that some people do not receive Christ as the greatest gift of all?

3) Do you receive Christ as the greatest gift of all? Are you truly thankful for his coming to earth?

Children's Activity

(Suggested supplies: Props to help reenact what took place the night Christ was born, ie. household items to stand in for gold, frankincense, myrrh, shepherd's clothing, etc.)

1) With your guidance, let your children get creative and reenact the night of baby Jesus' birth, complete with visits from the shepherds, the wise men, etc.

2) Discuss with your children the importance of Christ's birth and ask them if they know why Jesus was the greatest gift of all.

(Suggestion: Let one of your children say this prayer out loud.)

Prayer

Dear Jesus, thank you so much for coming to earth as a little baby. Thank you for becoming like one of us so that you could feel the hurts we feel and truly relate to all people. Thank you, Jesus, for being the salvation of the world!

Action Step

Perhaps take a digital photo of your children's reenactment of Christ's birth (the manger scene) and post it as a reminder to be deeply thankful for his arrival on earth.

Day 16

In everything give thanks?

"Rejoice always; pray without ceasing; in everything give thanks;
for this is God's will for you in Christ Jesus."
(I Thes. 5:16-18, NASB)

At first glance, I Thes. 5:18 doesn't seem to make much sense... "in everything give thanks." How can we be thankful when the tire goes flat on the way to work or when someone at school steals your lunch? But notice the verse doesn't say "Be thankful because bad things happen." It simply says "in everything give thanks" or be thankful even when things seem to go wrong.

We know that problems and difficulties will always be with us, at least while we're here on earth. But if we're willing, God can make something good out of a bad situation. Remember the story of Joseph in the book of Genesis? Although he faced some terrible trials, he decided to focus on the faithfulness of the Lord instead of the depth of his problems. Joseph apparently believed that everything would work out in the end. And God gave him peace because Joseph praised God in everything, even in the midst of life-threatening circumstances!

Let's Talk About It!

What good might come out of praising God in the midst of the following situations?

1) You're stuck in a traffic jam.

2) You learn that someone at school has been spreading lies about you.

3) The doctor tells you that you only have six months to live.

Children's Activity

(Suggested supplies: piece of yellow construction paper, safety pin, washable marker / pencil / or crayon, safety scissors)

What would you do if a toy you were playing with suddenly broke? (ie. Cry? Yell? Pout?) Do you have other toys? Well, let's make Jesus very happy by keeping a smile instead of a frown. Let's be thankful for all of the other toys you have!

1) Draw a "smiley face" on the yellow paper, then cut it out.

2) Have your mom or dad pin the smiley face on your shirt or backpack.

3) Over the next few days, wear the happy face as a reminder to "keep a smile" and be thankful, even when things don't go your way.

Prayer

Dear Jesus, please help me to be thankful and think about your goodness even when things don't always go the way I want.

Action Step

Adults: Let's take a cue from the children's activity and make 3 or 4 small "smiley faces." Place these in familiar places and over the next few days, when you see a happy face, check your attitude. Ask: Do I have an attitude of praise right now?

Day 17

A Time of Deliverance

"Then they cried to the Lord in their trouble, and he saved them from their distress; He sent out his word and healed them, and delivered them from destruction. Let them thank the Lord for his steadfast love, for his wonderful works to humankind. And let them offer thanksgiving sacrifices, and tell of his deeds with songs of joy." (Ps. 107: 19-22, NRSV)

It was a rainy August morning as I was headed to work in my little Plymouth Horizon. The eight-lane highway was packed with traffic as it was smack in the middle of the busy rush hour. The year was 1990. To be honest, I was probably going a bit too fast for the conditions and although I was in the far left lane (the passing lane), the car in front of me insisted on driving at what seemed like a snail's pace. I must also confess that I was following this car too closely. In fact, I was close enough to tell that the woman who was driving that car wasn't about to move over even though there was no room to pass her on the right. What happened next seems almost surreal, but it is also something I'll never forget.

The woman in front of me suddenly, unexpectedly, slammed on her brakes! As you might guess, because I (the genius) was following too close, I also had to slam hard on my brakes and quickly lost control of my car. My vehicle, which initially began to swerve, soon started spinning around in circles! Then, to make a desperate situation even worse, my car began to spin around in front of the other lanes, moving from the far left lane across the lanes of traffic to the right shoulder. I remember on the first spin, I came face to face with one of those enormous eighteen-wheelers. Then, I continued to spin across traffic until I came to a stop just off the highway, on the right shoulder!

A couple of commuters who witnessed all of this pulled over behind me. With bewildered expressions on their faces they asked me if I was alright. "Yes, I think so" I replied, still somewhat in a daze. I remember checking my body for any signs of injury and looking in the rear view mirror to see if I might be bleeding. When I realized I was physically okay, I got out and checked my little Horizon over, certain that it must have sustained at least a few dents, if not more damage. But there was nothing, not even a scratch! I was amazed; but beyond that, I knew without a doubt that God had spared my life. I also knew that I didn't deserve his mercy. Nevertheless, I was overwhelmed with gratitude!

That rainy day in August had a profound effect on me. Not only did I determine to drive more safely, but I also resolved within myself to much more earnestly fulfill God's calling upon my life. We may each have a unique part to play within his divine drama, but we must remember that God's call is universal: he has a collective plan that is intended to involve all of us! None of us deserves deliverance from troubles or calamities, but we offer sacrifices of thanksgiving knowing that he has greater plans for us, not to become kings and rulers, but to yield ourselves as instruments in his hands!

Let's Talk About It!

1) Can you recall a time when God delivered you out of a terrible situation?

2) What was your response when God spared you from additional harm?

3) Looking back, how do you feel about it now?

Children's Activity

If your children would like, using markers or crayons and paper, have them pictorially retell the story of Shadrach, Meshach, and Abednego and how they were rescued from King Nebuchadnezzar's fiery furnace. You may recall that the King had them thrown into the furnace because they refused to bow down and worship the King's enormous idol. (If you need more help, go to Daniel chapter 3.)

Prayer

Our Father and Provider, thank you for the many times you have protected us from unknown dangers and have rescued us from overwhelming troubles. Help us to never take your mercies for granted but live our lives as obedient children, yielded as earthen vessels in your hands.

Action Step

As a tangible act of gratitude for God's deliverance and loving kindness in our lives, consider rescuing an orphaned or destitute child in some troubled part of the world. There are some very legitimate and responsible organizations, such as God's Kids or World Vision, that can help your family sponsor one or more children who desperately need your help! What could be a more fitting recognition of God's mercy in our lives than to help a child out of the pit of despair? Beyond mere words, it's also a great way for your children to see your faith in action!

Day 18

Are you leading the praise band?

"Praise the Lord! Praise God in his sanctuary; praise him in his mighty firmament! Praise him for his mighty deeds; praise him according to his surpassing greatness! Praise him with trumpet sound; praise him with lute and harp! Praise him with tambourine and dance; praise him with strings and pipe! Praise him with clanging cymbals; praise him with loud clashing cymbals! Let everything that breathes praise the Lord! Praise the Lord!"
(Ps. 150, NRSV)

A few years ago my sister, Heidi, had some old 8mm home movies converted to VHS format in an effort to preserve our precious family memories. I remember one scene that showed my brother, Al, leading the high school marching band down Broadway in a local parade. There he was like a peacock, all decked out in his stunning red and white drum major's uniform, proudly strutting along, enthusiastically leading the way. Then the thought occurred to me, "It's got to inspire everyone in the band to be led by someone who's really into it, someone like my brother!"

In this life we know we'll certainly encounter good times as well as hard times. But do we make it a point to praise and thank God in *all* of our times? And beyond that, do we praise him enthusiastically? Like my brother, the drum major, do we inspire others to play their "instruments" with passion or lift their voices with zeal? Do others see us demonstrating an attitude of thanksgiving? Are we, in effect, leading the "praise band?"

Let's Talk About It!

1) Do others, such as your brothers and sisters, your parents, your children, your friends...do they see an attitude of praise in you? Or, do they witness a complaining, ungrateful spirit whenever you're around?

2) Although we all have times when we gripe or vent about something, has it become a habit with you?

3) Are you willing to change your attitude and become a leader when it comes to praise and thankfulness?

4) Will you be patient with others who are down in the dumps and pray that you might help them catch your infectious attitude of praise?

Children's Activity

Depending on the ages of your children, you could ask them to pretend they're leaders (like drum majors) of a big marching band. Using some common household or kitchen items as instruments, your family could play the part of the band while your kids lead the way! C'mon mom and dad, don't be like an old stick-in-the-mud! Have some fun with this! Lighten up, for Pete's sake, and have a good time. Your kids will and God will probably smile, too!

Prayer

Dear God, please help our family not let the world drag us down. Please help us to be the ones who choose to praise you and help us inspire other people to want to praise you, too! In Jesus name, Amen.

Action Step

Have your family think of a favorite praise and worship song. Why not make it a point to sing this song at least once each time you go somewhere together in the family vehicle? Try it, you'll like it!

Day 19

A New Song of Thanksgiving

"Praise the Lord with the lyre; make melody to Him with the harp of ten strings. Sing to Him a new song; play skillfully on the strings with loud shouts." (Ps. 33:2-3, NRSV)

Every year as the Christmas season winds down and New Year's Eve approaches, I find myself drawn into a time of reflection and reevaluation. I usually consider the events of the past year, the goals achieved or the opportunities missed, and tend to think about the time spent doing this or that and whether or not it was used wisely. I also tend to take stock of my energy reserves and whether or not I have the strength, and perhaps more importantly, the motivation to launch out into the new year with a renewed sense of purpose and enthusiasm.

Like me, I think many people thirst for fresh, new sources of inspiration. For it's not only rest that recharges our batteries, but a new outlook on things, a fresh wind that blows into our lives, a new source of inspiration! As amazing as it may sound, whenever I begin to sing or play music, I find my strength returning, my joy and optimism beginning to rise. A couple of days ago I was feeling very tired and even a bit gloomy; but, I whispered a word of thanks, sat down behind my drum set and began to play. Soon, almost inexplicably, my strength and joy returned! From a human standpoint, I should have dropped over from exhaustion, but I didn't!

Whenever we acknowledge God as the source of everything, the giver of life and every perfect gift, he inhabits our praise and blesses us in return. Don't misunderstand, we don't praise God with our voices or our instruments just so he will bless us, but when we are truly thankful for even the ability to praise him, something amazing happens... he does bless us! He gives us not only renewed strength, but a renewed vision, and a renewed sense of inspiration for the journey ahead. So as the Psalmist exclaimed: *Let everything that has breath praise the Lord!*

Let's Talk About It!

1) Do you awaken each day with a sense of excitement and a "new song" in your heart? Why or why not?

2) Do you live with a sense of anticipation, expecting God to work out his purposes in your life?

3) Do you thank God in advance for the "fresh wind" and renewed strength that he will provide in due time?

Children's Activity

Ask your child to think of a song she really likes that's new to her. Ask her what it is about the song that excites her and if she's willing, ask her to sing or hum the tune for everyone. Or, ask her to draw, paint, or color a picture that captures the inspiration of the song. Then, over the next day or two see if she'll sing the song again, or post her picture as a reminder that when we praise God with a new song of joy, he will give us a renewed sense of inspiration and strength.

Prayer

Dear Father, help us to realize that your mercies are new every morning and that you are continually redeeming creation for your purposes. Put a new song upon our lips that we may praise you with a fresh joy and gladness!

Action Step

Over the next few days, intentionally seek out new sources of inspiration, new reminders of the ongoing grace and creative work of God. Perhaps you could visit your local Christian bookstore and listen to some of the new praise and worship songs that have come out recently or visit a national park and drink in all of the wonderful sights and sounds. In any case, even in the midst of a disease-ridden, fallen world, reminders of God's overwhelming love are all around us, waiting to inspire us and fill our hearts with gratitude and praise!

Day 20

The Lord Dwells in the Hearts of Praise

"But You are holy, Who inhabit the praises of Israel."
(Ps. 22:3, NKJV)

I remember while growing up, adults at church would often ask us kids "Wouldn't you like to invite Jesus into your heart?" Now at first this puzzled me because as a small child I recall thinking *How can Jesus fit into my heart? Isn't he too big?* But it wasn't too long before I realized that Jesus can be anywhere... a big place, a small place, or anywhere in between... including my heart.

Today, during praise and worship time at our church, God's presence can be so powerful that I almost envision angels hovering above the congregation, joining us in glorifying the Lord. And I'm overwhelmed by the fact that the Creator of the universe, the great I Am actually lives in or inhabits the praises of his people! I can only imagine that He takes such delight, such pleasure, in hearing the loving affirmations of his people that He "jumps in with both feet" (to use a figure of speech).

So I guess one way to look at it is that if we really want our heavenly Father to live in our hearts, we better enjoy singing his praises... because scripture tells us that the holy One of Israel really does inhabit the praises of his people!

Let's Talk About It!
1) Do you ever feel God's presence in your heart when you praise him?

2) Has the realization that God actually lives in our praises ever dawned on you before?

3) At what times do you feel God's presence most in your heart?

Children's Activity
(Suggested supplies: Construction paper, crayons or washable markers, pencil, scissors)

1) On a light colored piece of construction paper, draw a heart to represent your own heart.

2) Now draw a picture of Jesus inside your heart (but make sure He looks happy).

3) Write words or melodies of praise coming from your heart.

Prayer

Heavenly Father, we do want you to live inside our hearts, so please help us to always praise you with all our love and devotion!

Action Step
With your parents' permission, post the picture somewhere convenient to remind you that God loves to live inside a heart of praise!

Day 21

Give thanks to God, not your lucky stars!

"It is good to give thanks to the Lord, And to sing praises to your name, O Most High; To declare Your loving kindness in the morning, And Your faithfulness every night..." (Ps. 92:1-2, NKJV)

One of many advantages I've had in teaching psychology has been to see how often science verifies the truth of God's word. For example, my wife recently forwarded me an email article by Jeff Myers, Ph. D. entitled *What's the Right Attitude in Times Like These?* This article cites research by Phil Graybeal who conducted a Spiritual Formation Audit (SFA) to "help Christian schools take their spiritual pulse." The question essentially being asked and answered by this research was "Do you know what virtue students, parents, and even school staff lacked the most... the virtue that is one of the top three character qualities psychologists say is essential to success in life... the virtue without which people lose hope, stop striving for worthy goals, and become bitter, angry, and defensive?" Well believe it or not, this virtue is simply *gratitude.*

In his book *The Psychology of Ultimate Concerns*, Robert Emmons discusses three virtues essential to success in life: self-control, humility, and of course, gratitude. According to Dr. Myers, Emmons defines gratitude as "The capacity to feel the emotion of thankfulness on a regular and consistent basis, across situations and over time." Ingratitude, on the other hand, operates out of a sense of entitlement that says *I have a right to have things go my way so that I can be happy.* Yet ironically, psychological research indicates again and again that people whose main pursuit is attaining money, fame, or beauty are consistently found to be less happy and less healthy than those who pursue less materialistic goals. In fact, several findings indicate that individuals who consistently demonstrate (articulate) gratitude report greater progress toward their goals than those who don't. Gratitude, it appears, not only increases optimism, it also increases productive activity.

As Christians we know that it takes more than just a general sense of gratitude, because without God as the primary recipient of our gratitude, life loses its fundamental purpose and meaning! Yet, even secular research validates what scripture has been telling us for thousands of years: that a thankful heart is a happy heart and that a joyful heart is good medicine! So, let's give thanks to God, not our lucky stars, for he is truly worthy of our thanks!

Let's talk About It!

1) How often do you count your blessings and then thank God for them?

2) Are you willing to thank Him everyday, even for the little things?

Children's Activity

(Suggested supplies: large piece of construction paper, magic marker, pen or pencil)

1) At the top of the construction paper, using the magic marker, write in large letters "I'm thankful for..."

2) Now, over the next several days, have each member of the family add to a numbered list things that each one is thankful for.

3) After adding something to the list, each person should write his/her name or initial. The list would look something like this:

I'm Thankful for...

1. My teddy bear – Timmy

2. Rainbows – Anna

3. A dry garage to park our car in – dad

4. Our wonderful church – mom

5. Your mom and my beautiful wife – dad

Prayer

{ *Dear God, thank you for the gift of gratitude.*
Thank you for blessing those who acknowledge you.
Help us to continually count our blessings! Amen.

Action Step

After about a week or so, check the list to see how many things have been added. Review the list and thank God for those blessings again! If your family chooses, you can continue to add to the list as a reminder to always count your blessings. The point to remember is that there are always things to be thankful for and that we should focus on those things. Otherwise, we might be tempted to dwell on what we don't have, becoming discontented and complaining!

Day 22

The Monthly Blessing Project

"Give and it will be given to you; good measure, pressed down, shaken together, and running over..." (Luke 6: 38, NKJV)

You might recall that day five of this devotional series, entitled "Expect A Blessing," dealt with the biblical principle that when we give to others or do something good for them, God blesses us in return. Yet, we need to emphasize the fact that we should never bless others just to get God to shower *us* with blessings! If that's our primary motivation, we're really missing the point, not to mention the fact that God looks on our hearts and if our motives are corrupt or impure, no blessing will be forthcoming.

Several years ago I took one of my daughters to see a movie entitled *Savannah Smiles,* a comedy about two hapless criminals who discover a little girl in the back seat of their stolen car. Savannah, the little girl, had evidently run away from home because she felt lonely and neglected, especially by her wealthy father. The two criminals, although clearly lawbreakers, were basically harmless and even developed a deep fondness and pure love for little Savannah. In one particularly poignant scene, the police had surrounded an abandoned house where the three runaways were hiding. The officers had their guns trained on one of the men and were about to shoot him when he lovingly reached down and picked up little Savannah, who was crying. As he held her close, drying her tears and comforting her, he had no idea that his act of kindness was effectively saving his life... for the sharpshooters were hesitant to fire since he was so close to the precious little girl.

I think in much the same way, when our motives are pure and we act out of a heart of love, we essentially are saving ourselves *from* ourselves. I say this because it's so easy to allow selfish ambition and selfish actions to destroy our lives. Instead, why not make blessing others a priority and enjoy the gift God brings when he uses us to make a difference in the life of someone else! Below is just one way to accomplish this... a practice our family calls *The Monthly Blessing Project*.

Let's Talk About It!

1) Do you know someone who could use your family's help, such as a neighbor, friend, or coworker?

2) Do you think it would please God for your family to bless another person or family each month?

Family Activity – The Monthly Blessing Project

1) First, come up with a simple calendar that will allow your family to keep track of who you choose to bless each month. Again, it could be someone you know, such as a neighbor or a family at your church, or it could be someone half-way around the world. As a family (kids included), talk about who you would like to bless first. Remember, this will be a different person or family each month.

2) Write down specific ways you plan to bless this person or family. You might decide, for example, that you would like to do something for this person or family once a week. You might even decide to tie your blessing to a traditional event or holiday occurring during that month. (e.g. One February, our daughters created some homemade valentines to which we attached some money and a few chocolates.)

3) Next, decide if you'll keep the blessing (the act of kindness) a secret. In other words, are you going to let the person or family know who's delivering the blessing? It might be better, in some cases, to keep your identity hidden... after all, you're not doing this because you expect a big 'thank you' in return! (See Matt. 6: 3-4)

4) Finally, remember that you don't need to spend a lot of money to conduct an effective blessing project! In fact, some of the best blessings may not have anything at all to do with money. That neighbor may be a senior citizen who hasn't been able to clean up her garage by herself. So... help her! Or, it may be a relative who's feeling lonely and forgotten. Send a card or letter with some pictures painted by your children, something to let that relative know that he or she is not forgotten!

Prayer

Father God... help us to always remember the simplicity of the golden rule and bless others as we would want to be blessed! Help us to not get so self-focused that we lose sight of the fact that people all around us are desperately in need of a real blessing.

Action Step

The only thing I would say here is to actually carry through with the project and intentionally bless someone each month. When you, as parents, involve your children in this activity, it will teach them a lesson about gratitude and giving that they likely will never forget (especially when they see *you* setting the example)!

Day 23

Let your life be a living thank you!

"For to me, to live is Christ, and to die is gain." (Phil. 1: 21, NKJV)

Recently when I was thinking about the people, other than my parents, who have had the greatest impact upon my life, one name in particular came to mind. His name was Larry Watson and he was our church's high school youth leader and choir director. Larry and his wife, Linda, were amazing people and both had a big influence on me, especially during those important teen years. But Larry had an especially profound impact on me... so profound, in fact, that it that endures to this day.

I guess you could say that Larry was one of those rare individuals who didn't just "talk the talk," he also "walked the walk." He lived a life of integrity and true Christian character in front of all of us everyday. A caring, dynamic individual that always expressed the joy of the Lord, Larry brought a group of 60 immature, selfish teenagers together and taught us what it means to be instruments of God. "Anything less than 100% for the Lord isn't good enough" was a phrase he'd often say. And more than anything else, his life was a living "thank you" to the heavenly Father.

A few years ago, after a long battle with stomach cancer, Larry went home to be with the Lord. But the impact that Larry had, not only upon that group of teens back in the '70s, but upon everyone he came in contact with, will never be forgotten. When a man's life is a living "thank you" to the Lord, you can be sure his impact will be felt not only in this lifetime, but down through the eons of eternity!

Let's Talk About It!

1) Do you know of someone like Larry whose life is a living "thank you?" If so, what is it about this person that makes him or her so dynamic?

2) Can you honestly echo the words of the apostle Paul and say "... to live is Christ, and to die is gain?"

Children's Activity

(Suggested supplies: medium size peel-and-stick name tags OR supplies of your parents' choice)

1) On the peel-and-stick name tags simply write the words "THANK YOU!"

2) Stick the tag on your shirt and when someone asks you "Who are you thanking and why?" just tell them you always want to remember to thank God *with* your life *for* your life!

Prayer

Father, please help each one of us remember to thank you with our lives. Help us remember to thank you with all that we are and all that we have... our time, talents, energy, and money... in other words, ourselves!

Action Step

Go to the people that most represent the Larry in your life and thank them for the impact they've had on you!

Day 24

Forever is a long time to praise the Lord!

"And there shall be no night there: They need no lamp nor light of the sun, for the Lord God gives them light. And they shall reign forever and ever." (Rev. 22: 5, NKJV)

It's absolutely amazing to think about a life that will have no end... a life spent in praise and adoration of the King of kings and Lord of lords! Not only that, but it's almost incomprehensible that this same majestic King would live with us and lovingly care for us for the rest of eternity. Listen to what *Rev. 21: 3-4* says when John writes: *Behold, the tabernacle of God is with men, and He will dwell with them, and they shall be His people, and God Himself will be with them and be their God. And God will wipe away every tear from their eyes; there shall be no more death, nor sorrow, nor crying; and there shall be no more pain, for the former things have passed away.*

I must admit that it almost brings tears of joy to my eyes to consider the goodness and undeserved love of God! When we think of all that the Lord has done and will do, praising Him forever won't be a chore... it will be an honor!

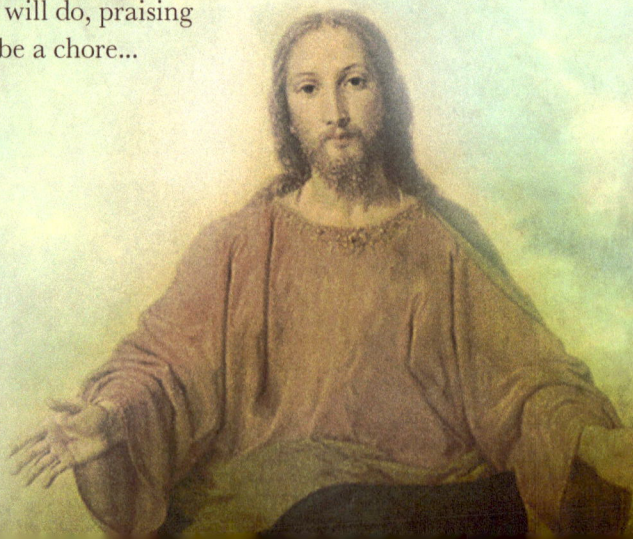

Let's Talk About It!

1) If someone gave you a million dollars, how thankful would you be? To what lengths would you go to show your gratitude to that person?

2) If someone saved your life, how much time do you think you'd spend thanking that individual?

3) In light of that, do you think it will be difficult praising God for all eternity?

Children's Activity

(Suggested supplies: plain white paper or construction paper, colored pencils / crayons or washable markers)

1) Ask your child to draw a picture of heaven with Jesus somewhere in the middle and families around him. Your child can also include angels, clouds, etc... whatever he/she thinks will be in heaven, too.

2) Now ask your child: "What do you think these families are saying or doing? Do you think they might be singing a praise song? If so, which one?"

Prayer

Our Savior, King, and Father... thank you for the promise of eternal life with you! Help us to never take this amazing gift for granted, and help us to always remember that life on earth is temporary and that our true home will be in heaven with you! In Jesus' name, Amen."

Action Step

Parents, please post your child's picture in a prominent place so that over the next few days everyone in the family can be reminded of our eternal destiny... a life with no end in heaven praising our Lord and King!

Day 25

Thanksgiving Remembrance: Five Kernels of Thanks

"...for I have learned in whatever state I am, to be content."
(Phil. 4: 11, NKJV)

It may be hard to believe, but here we are on the last day of this Thanksgiving devotional! Ideally, today will also be the official Thursday Thanksgiving Day holiday in your home. And as such, I'd like to share a family tradition that has taken on deep significance in the Lilienthal home, a tradition we simply call... *five kernels of thanks.*

When the Pilgrims landed in America in 1620, they found that first winter to be especially brutal. Food and supplies were very scarce and many died. It got so bad, in fact, that almost everyone was placed on a five-kernel-a-day ration of corn! Can you imagine... getting by on just five kernels of corn per day! (And we gripe when we run out of ice cream and potato chips!) But it's true. And although they seldom had little more than those five kernels of corn, they kept their faith and were grateful.

So, in honor of the pilgrims' sacrifice and spirit of gratitude, we at the Lilienthal household began a tradition many years ago using five kernels of corn to symbolize our thankfulness to God. We hope and pray that this ritual (or some version of it) will become a cherished tradition in your home, too, as you gather around the table and recall all of the blessings God has bestowed on your family throughout the year!

Thanksgiving Day Family Activity

As you gather around the table to partake of the traditional Thanksgiving meal, give each member of the family five kernels of "Indian corn" (you know, the hard, multi-colored kind). There should also be some kind of container placed in the middle of the table in which to put the kernels. (We use a small wicker-type basket, but almost anything will do.) Taking turns, go around the table and ask each family member to share something for which he or she is thankful. As each one shares, a kernel is placed in the center basket to represent his or her gift of gratitude. Eventually, each one will have shared five things he or she is thankful for as the fifth kernel of corn is placed in the basket. We also suggest that you have someone write down what each person is thankful for and review these each Thanksgiving Day.

In addition to being fun, this activity will take on a deeper level of meaning with each passing year. I say this because your children's offerings of gratitude will reflect deeper levels of spiritual maturity as they grow older. And as my wife Ronda and I grow older, our responses reflect an ever increasing awareness of God's goodness and faithfulness in both the mountain experiences and valleys of our lives. It is our prayer that your family will not only enjoy sharing this journey of gratitude each year, but that an attitude of thanksgiving will find a permanent place in your hearts!